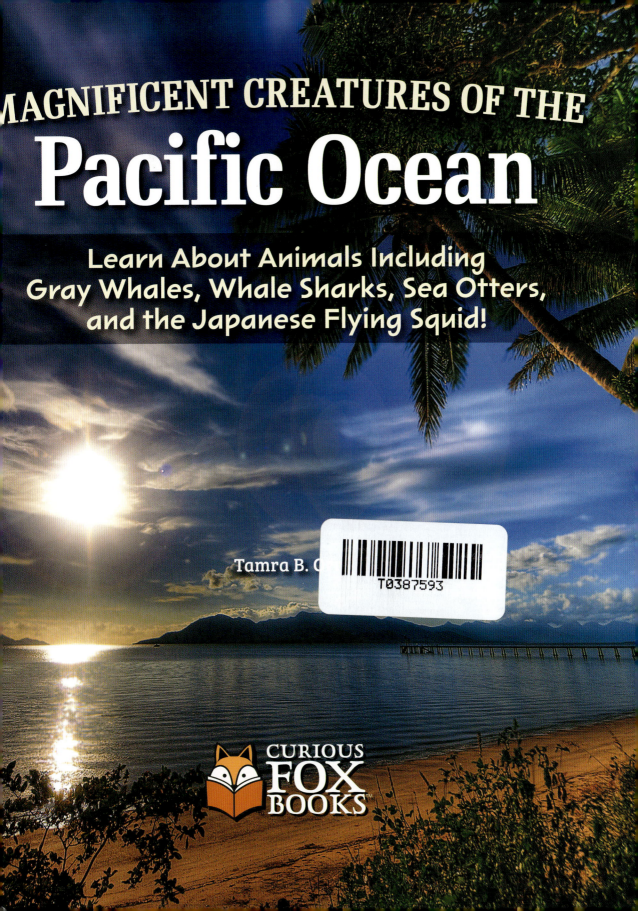

MAGNIFICENT CREATURES OF THE
Pacific Ocean

Learn About Animals Including Gray Whales, Whale Sharks, Sea Otters, and the Japanese Flying Squid!

Tamra B. O.

CURIOUS FOX BOOKS

ASIA

NORTH AMERICA

PACIFIC OCEAN

SOUTH AMERICA

AUSTRALIA

The average depth from the Pacific Ocean's surface to its floor is over 2 miles (3.2 kilometers). That's the length of about 35 football fields!

Welcome to the Pacific (puh-SIH-fik) Ocean, the world's biggest ocean. It covers over 63 million square miles (163.2 million square kilometers). If every piece of land on the planet were laid on top of this ocean, there would still be room left over. Three quarters of the world's volcaones are found around the Pacific Ocean. Powerful volcanoes often given birth to new islands, especially near Japan. The Pacific Ocean has more than 25,000 islands.

The Pacific Ocean is full of trenches (TRENTCHS), which are very deep cuts in the ocean floor. The Pacific's Mariana (mar-ee-AH-na) Trench is the deepest in the world. It is deeper than Mount Everest is tall.

One of the creatures that can be found deep in the ocean is the dumbo octopus. These are a type of deep-sea umbrella octopus with fins that resemble elephant ears. They use the fins to move through the water, steering with their webbed arms.

The first trip to explore the deepest part of the Mariana Trench (known as Challenger Deep) was in 1960 when two men rode down in a research submarine (bathyscape) called the *Trieste*.

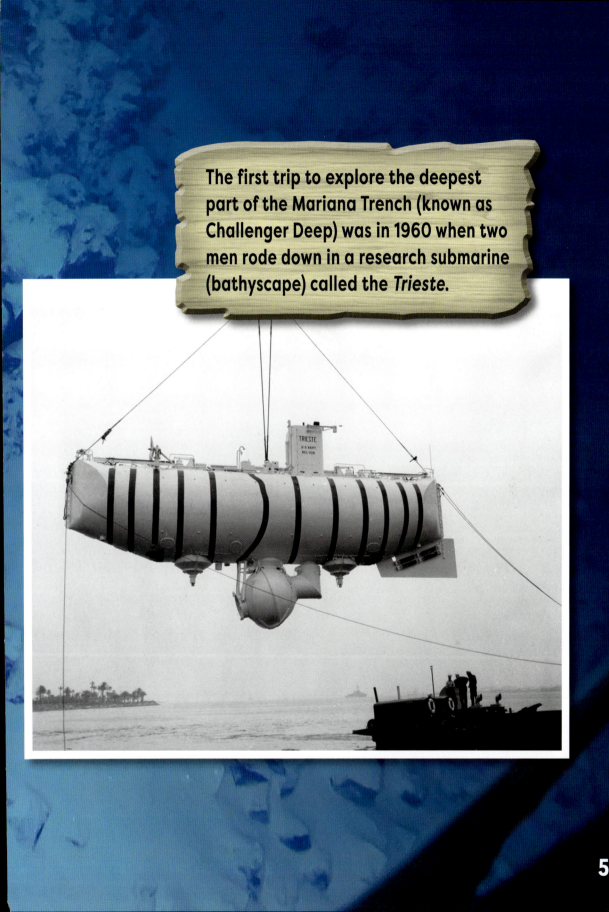

The Pacific Ocean has huge mats of green or brown kelp, known as the forests of the sea. These thick plants slow down the ocean currents **(KUR-rents)** and are important parts of the ocean. Kelp grows very fast, up to 24 inches (61 centimeters) a day!

When baby sea otters are born, their mothers will often groom them for hours. Otter pups have dense fur that causes them to float. Around 13 weeks later, they start to get their adult fur and begin to learn how to dive and hunt from their mothers.

　Sea otters are known to be a "keystone species" for kelp forests. This means they keep the forests balanced by eating just the right amount of the small creatures like urchins that live in the kelp. Groups of male or female sea otters form "rafts," with male rafts being larger than female rafts. These groups live in the kelp forests and wrap themselves in the kelp when they rest to keep from floating away.

Just off the coast of Australia is the Pacific Ocean's biggest coral reef: the Great Barrier Reef (**greyt BAR-ee-er REEF**). Made up of thousands of corals, it is so huge that it can actually be seen from space! It's actually the largest living structure on Earth.

Corals look like rocks, but they're actually made up of tiny creatures called polyps. A coral reef's bright colors come from algae that live on the coral.

Blue sea stars live in the Great Barrier Reef. They move slowly through the water. Sea stars have their mouths in the middle of their undersides, and they use this to trap their prey.

Giant clams also live in coral reefs. Their mantles (the frilly bits that stick out of their shells) are also home to the algae they eat. They open their shells wide during the day so the algae can get the light it needs.

Around the edges of coral reefs in the Pacific Ocean, you might see the large fish known as the humphead wrasse, Maori wrasse, or Napoleon fish. These fish can grow over 6 feet (1.8 meters) long. They eat a lot of creatures that normally hide under the sand, so they sometimes dig for food or rely on stingrays to help dig.

The spotted eagle ray is one of the largest of the Pacific's rays. These rays often swim near the ocean's surface and have huge wingspans. They can grow up to 10 feet (3.1 meters) wide! Spotted eagle rays have flat teeth that it uses to crush and grind the shells of some of its favorite prey. It has a long whip-like tail with venomous barbed spines at the base.

The Japanese flying squid lives in the northern Pacific Ocean. These squids can perform something like jet propulsion. If they are chased, they can take in water and push it out with enough force to leap out of the water over 150 feet (45.7 meters)!

Walruses (WOLL-ruh-ses) live along the Pacific's shores. They weigh up to 3,700 pounds (1,678.3 kilograms), which is as much as a car. They have 400–700 large whiskers that are supplied with blood and are very sensitive. They use their whiskers to find food along the sandy ocean floor.

Walrus tusks can grow to more than 3 feet (91.4 centimeters) long. They use them to fight, pull themselves out of the water, and punch breathing holes in the ice.

Walruses are social animals. Mothers take care of their babies for up to five years, and adults often form large groups. A group of walruses can even generate fog because it gets so hot!

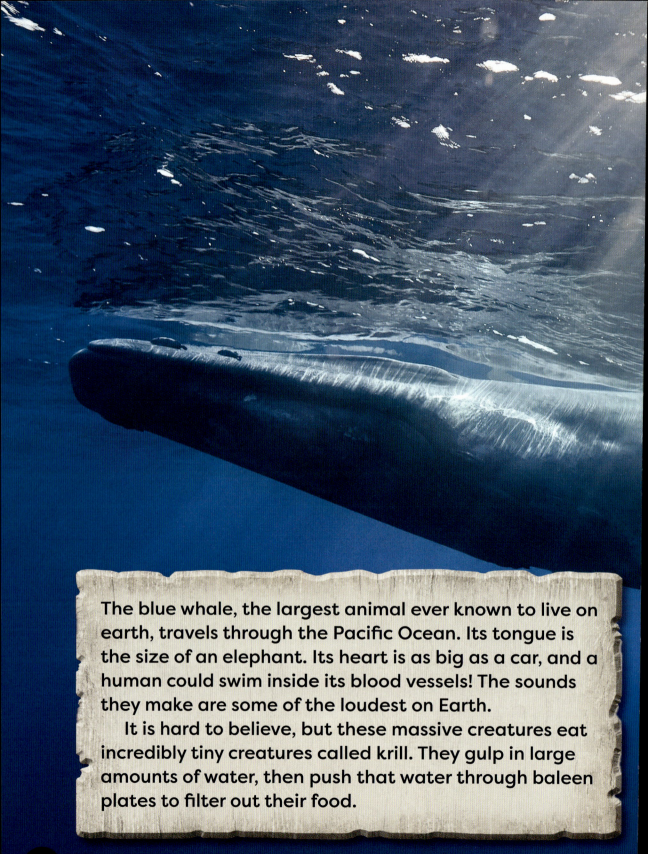

The blue whale, the largest animal ever known to live on earth, travels through the Pacific Ocean. Its tongue is the size of an elephant. Its heart is as big as a car, and a human could swim inside its blood vessels! The sounds they make are some of the loudest on Earth.

It is hard to believe, but these massive creatures eat incredibly tiny creatures called krill. They gulp in large amounts of water, then push that water through baleen plates to filter out their food.

The endangered (en-DAYN-jerd) gray whale migrates through the Pacific Ocean, too. They travel more than 10,000 miles (16,093.4 kilometers) each year.

The Pacific Ocean is home to many different types of seals. One that loves the warmer waters around the Hawaiian islands is the Hawaiian monk seal. There are only around 1,500 Hawaiian monk seals in the world. These seals spend most of their time hunting or basking in the sun on Hawaiian beaches and rocks.

Ribbon seals are born on ice in the Northern Pacific Ocean in the spring. They are white as pups, but end up with ribbon-like stripes as adults. These seals are rare to see since they usually live in the open ocean.

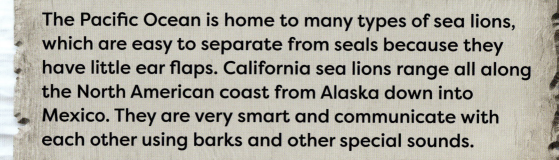

The Pacific Ocean is home to many types of sea lions, which are easy to separate from seals because they have little ear flaps. California sea lions range all along the North American coast from Alaska down into Mexico. They are very smart and communicate with each other using barks and other special sounds.

The Galápagos Islands, in the Pacific Ocean off the coast of Ecuador, are known for having many special animals. The Galápagos sea lion is just one. These sea lions are smaller than their Californian cousins.

The most common shark in the Pacific Ocean is the blacktip reef shark. They prefer shallow waters and coral reefs. It is easy to recognize them because of the black tips on their fins. They can be timid and usually avoid people. When they are first born, they often form large groups in areas that have been flooded by high tides.

The largest fish in the Pacific Ocean (and on Earth) is the whale shark. These huge sharks move slowly through the water, filtering out tiny plankton (**PLANK-tin**) for food.

One of the unusual creatures you can find in the Pacific Ocean is the chambered nautilus. These creatures are like living fossils—they haven't changed in 150 million years! Each one has a chambered shell and more than 90 sticky tentacles that extend out. As the chambered nautilus gets older, it will build more chambers, and its stripes spread out over the surface. They move by using a siphon to push water out in different directions.

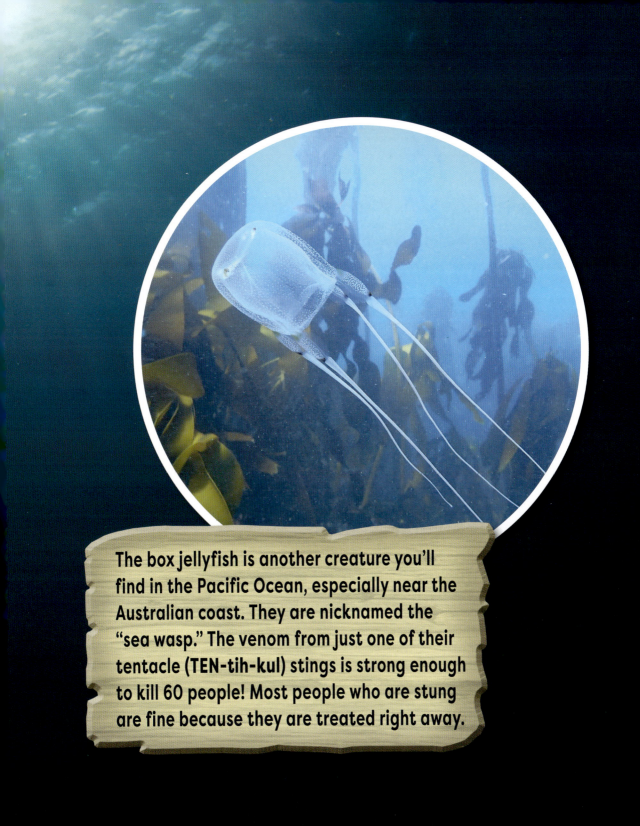

The box jellyfish is another creature you'll find in the Pacific Ocean, especially near the Australian coast. They are nicknamed the "sea wasp." The venom from just one of their tentacle (TEN-tih-kul) stings is strong enough to kill 60 people! Most people who are stung are fine because they are treated right away.

The Pacific Ocean's oddest creatures live thousands of feet down in the darkest, coldest waters.

The fangtooth is a frightening dark-colored fish. Because its teeth are so long and sharp, it can't close its mouth normally. Its teeth slide into special pouches to keep them from poking into its brain.

Most female anglerfish have rods on their heads with glowing tips that lure in their prey in the dark ocean. The rod also attracts male anglerfish, which are very small and live on female anglerfish like parasites.

Fangtooths may look scary, but they're not dangerous to people. They are small and they avoid light. They only come into the upper layers of the ocean at night.

The glowing tip on an anglerfish's rod is a small organ filled with millions of bacteria that produce light.

The Pacific Ocean is necessary to many marine and island birds, too. One of the most common is the California brown pelican, which is known for its large pouch. A pelican's pouch is underneath its bill and can hold up to 3 gallons (11.4 liters) of water and dozens of fish. The water drains out, and then the pelicans swallow the fish in one big gulp.

Almost half of the world's water is in the Pacific Ocean. It is an amazing place, full of life and wonder that needs to be protected.

The blue-footed booby is another one of the amazing animals found on the Pacific Ocean's Galápagos Islands. The blue color in their feet comes from the nutrients in the fish they eat. The brighter the blue, the healthier the bird.

FURTHER READING

Books

Callery, Sean. *Life Cycles: Ocean*. New York: Kingfisher, 2012.

Gonzales, Doreen. *The Huge Pacific Ocean*. Berkeley Heights, NJ: Enslow Elementary, 2013.

Pledger, Maurice. *Sounds of the Wild: Ocean*. San Diego: Silver Dolphin Books, 2008.

Spilsbury, Louise, and Richard Spilsbury. *Pacific Ocean*. Portsmouth, NH: Heinemann, 2015.

Web Sites

Kids World Travel Guide: Pacific Ocean
   https://www.kids-world-travel-guide.com/pacific-ocean-facts.html

Science Kids: Oceans
   https://www.sciencekids.co.nz/sciencefacts/earth/oceans.html

World Wildlife Fund: Oceans
   https://www.worldwildlife.org/initiatives/oceans

GLOSSARY

current (KUR-rent)—An area of water that moves in one direction.

endangered (en-DAYN-jerd)—Under the threat of extinction.

Great Barrier Reef (greyt BARee-er REEF)—The biggest coral reef in the Pacific Ocean, made up of thousands of corals.

kelp (KELP)—A type of green or brown seaweed.

Mariana Trench (mar-ee-AH-na TRENTCH)—The deepest trench in the Pacific Ocean.

plankton (PLANK-tin)—Tiny organisms that live in the water.

ray (RAY)—A type of fish with a flat body and large fins that work like wings in the water.

tentacle (TEN-tih-kul)—A long, flexible body part, usually used for touch.

trench (TRENTCH)—A long, narrow cut in the ground.

tusk (TUSK)—An extremely long tooth found in creatures, such as elephants and walruses.

volcanoes (vol-KAYnoh-s)—Openings in the earth's crust where lava, volcanic ash, and gases escape.

walruses (WOLL-ruh-ses)—Huge marine mammals that have wide heads, small eyes, whiskers, and two large, downward-pointing tusks.

PHOTO CREDITS

p. 1—Paul Bica; pp. 4-5—Vlvescovo; pp. 6-7—Shutterstock/David A Litman; p. 6 (inset)—Shutterstock/Alaskan Wildlife; pp. 8-9—Shutterstock/Alexandre.ROSA; p. 9 (inset)—Shutterstock/blue-sea.cz; pp. 10-11—Shutterstock/Tanya Puntti; p. 10 (inset)—Shutterstock/Jenifer DeLemont; pp. 12-13—Shutterstock/Longjourneys; p. 13 (inset)—Shutterstock/Shpatak; p. 14 (inset)—US Geological Survey, KerryInLondon; pp. 16-17—Shutterstock/Ajit S N; p. 17 (inset)—NOAA; pp. 18-19—Shutterstock/Pamela Au; p. 19 (inset)—Jomillio75; pp. 20-21—Shutterstock/Dogora Sun; p. 20 (inset)—Shutterstock/Brian Lasenby; pp. 22-23—Shutterstock/Batuhan Nuri GANIZ; p. 23 (inset)—Shutterstock/blueplanet97; pp. 24-25—Shutterstock/Alex Permiakov; p. 25 (inset)—Shutterstock/Katherine Wallis; p. 26 (inset)—Citron; p. 27 (inset)—Shutterstock/Kan Sukarakan; pp. 26-27—Shutterstock/Nikolay_Alekhin; p. 29 (inset)—Shutterstock/CSNafzger. All other photos—Public Domain.

INDEX

Anglerfish 26, 27
Blue sea stars 9
Blue-footed boobies 29
Box jellyfish 25
Chambered nautilus 24–25
Coral 8, 9, 10, 11, 22
Dumbo octopus 4
Fangtooth fish 26
Galápagos Islands 20
Giant clams 10

Great Barrier Reef 8, 9
Hawaiian monk seals 18–19
Humphead wrasse 10–11
Japanese flying squid 13
Kelp 6, 7
Mariana Trench 4, 5
Ocean currents 6
Pacific Ocean
    borders 4
    size 2, 3

Pelicans 28
Ribbon seals 19
Sea lions 20–21
Sea otters 6–7
Sharks 22, 23
Spotted eagle ray 12–13
Walruses 14–15
Whales 16–17
Volcanoes 3, 4

© 2025 by Curious Fox Books™, an imprint of Fox Chapel Publishing Company, Inc.

Magnificent Creatures of the Pacific Ocean is a revision of *Water Planet: Life in the Pacific Ocean*, originally published in 2018 by Purple Toad Publishing, Inc. Reproduction of its contents is strictly prohibited without written permission from the rights holder.

Paperback ISBN 979-8-89094-170-1
Hardcover ISBN 979-8-89094-171-8

Library of Congress Control Number: 2024950039

To learn more about the other great books from Fox Chapel Publishing, or to find a retailer near you, call toll-free at 800-457-9112 or visit us at *www.FoxChapelPublishing.com*.
You can also send mail to:
Fox Chapel Publishing
903 Square Street
Mount Joy, PA 17552

We are always looking for talented authors. To submit an idea, please send a brief inquiry to acquisitions@foxchapelpublishing.com.

Fox Chapel Publishing makes every effort to use environmentally friendly paper for printing.

Printed in China